LEMMINGS

A TRUE BOOK®

by
Ann O. Squire

Children's Press®
A Division of Scholastic Inc.

New York Toronto London Auckland Sydney
Mexico City New Delhi Hong Kong
Danbury, Connecticut

A Norway lemming by the side of a road

Content Consultant
Kathy Carlstead, PhD
Research Scientist
Honolulu Zoo

Reading Consultant
Cecilia Minden-Cupp, PhD
Former Director, Language and
Literacy Program
Harvard Graduate School of
Education

Author's Dedication
For Evan

The photograph on the cover shows a Norway lemming. The photograph on the title page shows a collared lemming in the winter.

Library of Congress Cataloging-in-Publication Data
Squire, Ann.
   Lemmings / by Ann O. Squire.
     p. cm. — (A True Book)
   Includes bibliographical references and index.
   ISBN-10: 0-516-25470-7 (lib. bdg.)   0-516-25581-9 (pbk.)
   ISBN-13: 978-0-516-25470-8 (lib. bdg.)   978-0-516-25581-1 (pbk.)
   1. Lemmings—Juvenile literature. I. Title. II. Series.
QL737.R666S69 2006
599.35'82—dc22   2005003273

Contents

A Norway lemming feeds on grass.

A Very Unusual Mammal

The word *lemmings* makes many people think of odd little creatures traveling in masses to the sea. As thousands of lemmings head to water, many die by drowning in lakes or rivers or by falling off cliffs. This behavior has been a mystery for years.

5

People have offered many different explanations for this strange behavior. As we'll learn later, scientists still aren't entirely sure of the answer. But lemmings are interesting animals to study just the same.

Lemmings are the smallest **mammals** in the Arctic, measuring about 5 inches (13 centimeters) long. They live in the most northern parts of Canada, Scandinavia, Greenland, and Russia. In these places, the temperature is below

Lemmings are the Arctic's smallest mammals.

32 degrees Fahrenheit
(0 degrees Celsius) for much
of the year.

Unlike many other Arctic
animals, lemmings do not
spend the winter in a resting
state, or **hibernate**. Nor do
they have a thick layer of fat
to protect them from the
cold. Lemmings do have a
number of special features
called **adaptations** that help
them to survive in the harsh
northern climate.

The lemming has small ears and a short tail.

One adaptation to the cold is the lemming's very short ears, legs, and tail. These parts of the body lose heat the most quickly. Because they are short, however, the animal stays warm.

Another adaptation is their fur. A lemming's fur is long and dense. It repels water, keeping the animal warm and dry.

One kind, or **species**, of lemming is the collared lemming. These lemmings shed their coats in the fall and grow winter coats that are pure white. The white fur helps to hide the lemmings from snowy owls, Arctic foxes, and other animals looking in the white snow for lemmings to eat.

The collared lemming changes its coat from grayish brown (top) to white in the winter (bottom).

Life on the Tundra

The treeless plains where most lemmings live are covered with snow for many months of the year. This land is called **tundra**. The ground underneath the tundra is always frozen. This layer of soil is called **permafrost**. This frozen layer of soil prevents

Tundra land is often covered with snow. The ground underneath is always frozen.

the lemmings from digging deep burrows to keep warm.

Lemmings make their nests under the snow.

You might think that, under such harsh conditions, these little animals would find it difficult to stay alive. The truth is that snow is the key to their survival.

Lemmings live in the space just underneath the snow during the winter. They look for food and make their grassy nests there. The thick blanket of snow above their heads actually helps protect them from the cold weather outside.

Even with this layer of protection, the lemmings' home is not exactly warm. Temperatures beneath the snow are usually around −10°F (−23°C).

Lemmings eat grass and other plants. That makes them **herbivores**. They feed on grasses, leaves, twigs, and bark as well as moss, berries, and even pine needles. These foods are easy enough to find in the summertime. Things are more difficult in the winter,

Lemmings feed on grass and other plants.

and the lemmings must
search underneath the snow
for plant growth to eat.

For the winter, the collared lemming grows strong claws on its front feet.

Some lemmings have large, flattened claws. They use these big claws to dig through the snow.

The collared lemming has normal claws during the summer. For the winter, the collared lemming grows two strong claws on each of its front feet. Some people in the Arctic have reported seeing lemmings using these powerful claws to dig through igloo ice!

Lots of Little Lemmings

Like mice and rats, lemmings are **rodents**. Rodents are small mammals with large, sharp front teeth that they use for gnawing.

Rodents are known for having many babies, but lemmings may just win the prize for being the youngest parents. Lemmings

A group of baby lemmings sleep close together.

are ready to mate and have babies when they are only a few weeks old.

A lemming mother takes care of her litter in the nest.

Another prize the lemmings might win is for having the largest rodent families. Lemmings mate and have babies from spring to fall.

A female lemming will give birth two to three weeks after mating. Each litter can have as many as thirteen young. Because a female can give birth to several litters during the summer, it is possible for a lemming to have as many as fifty babies in a single year.

Sometimes there will be good weather and plenty of food in the summer for the lemmings. Then the number of lemmings on the tundra will explode. These times are called lemming years. They seem to happen about once every four years.

In the years after a lemming year, the lemming population falls dramatically. Some summers, it is hard to find even one lemming in an area that

Lemming years occur when food is plentiful, as it is for these two Norway lemmings.

was home to hundreds of these animals just a few years before.

Scientists are not certain why lemming populations go up and down so much. People have suggested all kinds of reasons, such as widespread disease and changes in the weather.

Some people think the amount of available food explains population changes. There is a lot of competition for food during lemming years. Many grasses and other plants are wiped out. Soon lemmings have little to eat. They may have fewer babies or even starve. The

Food for lemmings on the tundra can be sparse after a lemming year.

next year, because there are fewer lemmings, the plants can grow back. That may give rise to another lemming year.

Mysterious Migration

We may never know for sure what causes lemming years. Whatever the cause, a population explosion can have a strange effect on lemmings, especially the Norway lemming species. These animals become restless as their numbers grow.

Norway lemmings turn aggressive as their numbers increase.

Fights break out, and in time some lemmings leave in search of a less crowded home. More and more lemmings join them. A small movement turns into a huge migration.

Norway lemmings tend to travel down to lower forests. They often encounter large lakes, fast-flowing rivers, and rocky cliffs along the way. They are eager to get away from their overcrowded conditions.

A Norway lemming tries to make its way across a river.

Some lemmings may die trying to swim across lakes that are too wide or across rivers whose strong current carries them downstream. Crowds of lemmings may accidentally push others off cliffs.

Some people who have seen these migrations think that the lemmings are trying to kill themselves to solve the problem of overcrowding. It is true that thousands of lemmings may die on their long migrations. But most scientists today agree that these deaths are accidents.

Dead lemmings lie on the ground after a migration.

Staging the Arctic

A real herd of lemmings migrating

In 1958, a Disney nature movie called *White Wilderness* won an Academy Award for the year's best documentary. The film supposedly showed a huge herd of lemmings in the Canadian Arctic. The herd was shown to be killing themselves by jumping off cliffs into the sea. *White Wilderness* was largely responsible for people at that time believing that lemmings march to their deaths when their population grows too large.

What people didn't know was that the scene in *White Wilderness* was a fake. The movie used just a few dozen lemmings, and the animals did not jump. The filmmakers pushed them off the ledge! Although a spokeswoman from Disney couldn't confirm this story, she explained, "Staging wilderness scenes to make them look better was a common practice in the fifties."

An Arctic film crew at work in Canada today

Dangerous Living

While migrations are dangerous, life at home is not much
safer for lemmings. Many
animals on the Arctic tundra
feed on lemmings. They are
a main food source for snowy
owls, ravens, Arctic foxes,
wolves, weasels, and ermine.
A lemming's life is especially

A snowy owl brings a lemming to feed to her chicks.

dangerous in the summer, when it cannot hide under the snow.

Lemmings are very impor-
tant to the tundra **ecosystem**.
An ecosystem is a group of
animals and plants together
with the environment they live
in. Lemmings are important
to their ecosystem because
so many different animals
depend on them as food.

In lemming years, many
Arctic animals feast on these
little rodents. Eating lemmings
gives these animals the energy
they need to raise and feed

Lemmings are an important part of the tundra ecosystem.

Lemmings are a food source for many animals on the tundra, including the Arctic fox.

their young. But in years when lemmings are few, wolves, foxes, and other animals that feed on lemmings have trouble finding enough to eat. They may have fewer young or even starve to death as a result.

Lemmings face another danger as winter approaches. If freezing rain and frost come before the first snowfall, the grasses will be covered with ice. The lemmings will have nothing to eat.

If the weather turns bitterly cold before snow covers the ground, the lemmings are in danger of freezing to death. The lemmings need a blanket of snow to protect them and keep them warm.

Lemmings face many hardships. It is amazing that lemmings can survive at all. But as lemming years show us, this little rodent species not only stays alive, but it outnumbers most other animals on the tundra.

The Arctic's smallest mammal manages to survive on the tundra.

To Find Out More

Here are some additional resources to help you learn more about lemmings:

 **Books**

Kalman, Bobbie. **What Is a Rodent?** Crabtree Publishing, 2000.

Miller, Sara Swan. **Rodents: From Mice to Muskrats**. Franklin Watts, 1998.

Souza, D. M. **What's a Lemming?** Carolrhoda Books, 1998.

Walsh Shepherd, Donna. **Tundra**. Franklin Watts, 1996.

Woods, Samuel G., and Jeff Cline (illustrator). **The Amazing Book of Mammal Records: The Largest, the Smallest, the Fastest, and Many More!** Blackbirch Press, 2000.

⚡ Organizations and Online Sites

Alpine Biome
http://www.blueplanetbiomes.org/tundra.htm

This site provides information about the tundra's wildlife and climate.

Arctic Studies Center
http://www.mnh.si.edu/arctic/html/lemming.html

Check out this site for more information about the lemming and links to other Arctic sites.

Arctic Wildlife
http://www.saskschools.ca/~gregory/arctic/Awildlife.html

This site run by students in Saskatchewan provides easy-to-understand information about the lemming and many other Arctic animals.

Hinterland Who's Who
350 Michael Cowpland Drive
Kanata, Ontario
K2M 2W1 Canada
613-599-9594
http://www.hww.ca/hww2.asp?id=91

A partnership between the Canadian Wildlife Federation and the Canadian Wildlife Service, Hinterland Who's Who offers in-depth descriptions of lemmings and other wildlife, discussions on issues, actions that you can take to help wildlife, and educational materials.

Lemming
http://www.adfg.state.ak.us/pubs/notebook/smgame/lemmings.php
This site of the Alaska Department of Fish & Game Wildlife Notebook Series describes the different kinds of lemmings that live in Alaska.

Important Words

adaptations physical features or behaviors that help animals to survive better where they live

ecosystem a group of animals and plants together with the environment they live in

herbivores animals that feed on plants

hibernate to spend winter in a resting state

mammals warm-blooded animals that nurse their young

permafrost the layer of soil underneath tundra land that is always frozen

rodents small mammals with large, sharp front teeth used for gnawing

species a group of animals that have similar characteristics and a common name

tundra treeless plains between the ice cap and the timberline of North America, Europe, and Asia

Index

Meet the Author

Ann O. Squire has a PhD in animal behavior. Before becoming a writer, she spent several years studying African electric fish and the special signals they use to communicate with each other. Dr. Squire is the author of many books on natural science and animals, including *Beluga Whales*, *Moose*, *Penguins*, *Polar Bears*, and *Puffins*. She lives with her family in Katonah, New York.

Photographs © 2007: Animals Animals/Mark Chappell: 1, 11 bottom; Corbis Images/Dan Guravich: 35; Dembinsky Photo Assoc./Scott T. Smith: 13; Durham Photography/Michael Durham: 9; Minden Pictures: 27 (Tui De Roy), 37 (Michio Hoshino), 29, 31, 33 (Solvin Zankl/Foto Natura); Nature Picture Library Ltd.: 39 (Mike Potts), 2, 25 (Solvin Zankl); NHPA/Paal Hermansen: cover; Peter Arnold Inc.: 18 (BIOS), 17 (Fred Bruemmer), 7 (Georges Dif); Photo Researchers, NY: 34 (Jim Cartier), 21, 22 (Tom McHugh); Photolibrary.com: 11 top (Daniel Cox/OSF), 14 (Richard and Julia Kemp/OSF), 43 (Owen Newman/OSF); Superstock, Inc./age fotostock: 4; Visuals Unlimited/Tom Walker: 40.